Bond
SERIOUS ABOUT CHILDREN'S LEARNING

No Nonsense
Maths

5-6 years

Central pull-out pages

Parents' notes	A1
Answers	A2-4

Contents

Lesson

1	Numbers to 5	2
2	Addition to 5	4
3	Subtraction to 5	6
4	Addition facts to 5	8
5	2D shapes	10
6	Patterns	12
7	Comparing measures	14
8	Time – days and seasons	16

How am I doing?   18

9	Numbers to 10	20
10	Addition to 10	22
11	Subtraction to 10	24
12	Knowing when to add or subtract to 10	26
13	Addition facts to 10	28
14	Doubles and halves	30
15	First or last, more or less	32
16	3D shapes	34
17	Time – o'clock	36
18	Solving problems	38

How am I doing?   40

19	Reading and writing numbers to 20	42
20	Ordering numbers to 20	44
21	Tens and units	46
22	Counting in steps of 1 and 10	48
23	1 or 10 more or less	50
24	Counting in steps to 20	52
25	Odd and even numbers to 20	54
26	Number sequences	56
27	Estimating	58
28	Time – half past	60

How am I doing?   62

Try the 6–7 years book   64

www.bond11plus.co.uk

Numbers to 5

Look at the numbers. They go up in **order**.

1. **a** Colour 3 fish.

b Colour 2 fish.

c Colour 4 fish.

2. **Draw the fish.**

a

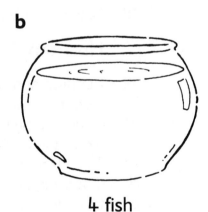

3 fish

b

4 fish

c

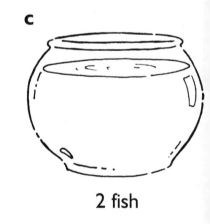

2 fish

3. **How many fish are in each bowl?**

a _____

b _____

c _____

4. Join the dots to make 4 shapes. Start on 1 each time. Use a ruler.

a
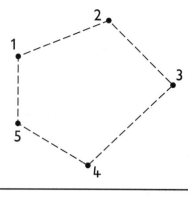

b
2

1   3
4

c
3   4

2

1 5

d
4

3   5
1

2

5. Fill in the missing numbers.

a 1   2   ____   4   5

b 1   2   3   ____   5

c ____   2   3   4   5

d ____   2   3   4   ____

How did I do?

Total

17

More practice? Go to www

1	2	3	4	5

Look at the number line.

a Which number comes after 3? ____

b Which number comes before 2? ____

c Which number comes after 4? ____

3

Addition to 5

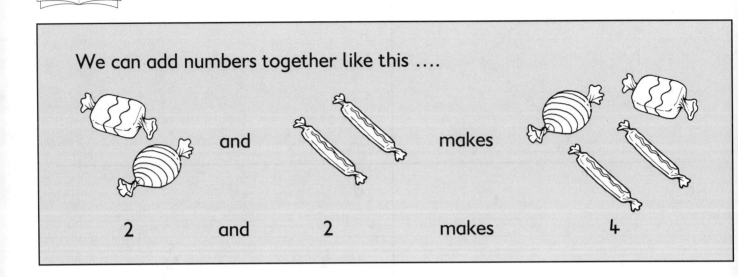

We can add numbers together like this ....

| 2 | and | 2 | makes | 4 |

1. Write the missing number in each gap.

a and makes 3

b and makes 5

c and makes 2

Now we will use the correct signs ... + and =.

2. Write the numbers in the gaps.

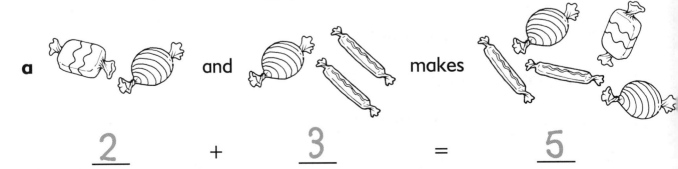

a and makes

2 + 3 = 5

b  and 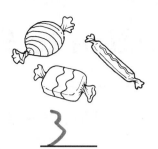 makes

$$\underline{1} + \underline{3} = \underline{4}$$

c  and  makes

$$\underline{3} + \underline{2} = \underline{5}$$

d 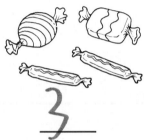 and makes

$$\underline{3} + \underline{1} = \underline{5}$$

3. **Add the numbers.**

   a $2 + 2 = \underline{4}$ **b** $4 + 1 = \underline{5}$

   c $3 + 1 = \underline{4}$ **d** $2 + 3 = \underline{5}$

How did I do?	☹	😐	😊

Total $\frac{100}{9}$

More practice? Go to www

More practice? Go to www

Challenge yourself

Write the answers.

a Tom has 1 sweet. Ann gives him 2 more.
   How many sweets does Tom now have? __3__

b What is the total of 3 and 2? __5__

c What must you add to 4 to make 5? __1__

Subtraction to 5

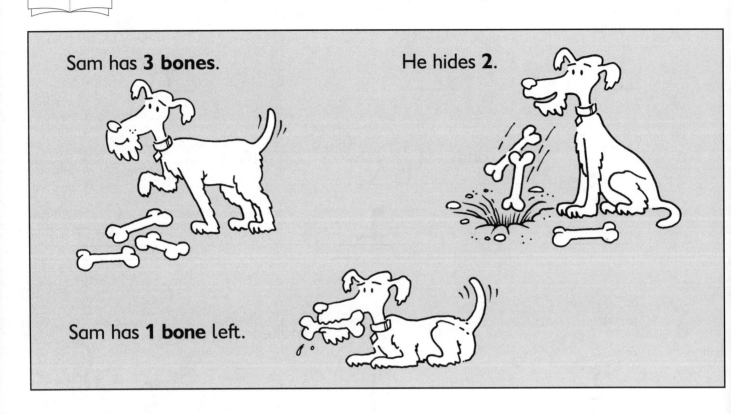

Sam has **3 bones**.

He hides **2**.

Sam has **1 bone** left.

1. **If you take away 2 bones from Sam how many will he have left?**

a  2

b 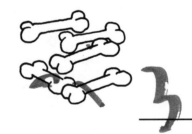 3

c 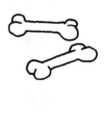 0

Now take away 3 bones.

d 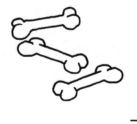 0

e 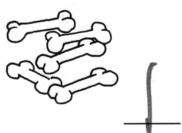 1

f 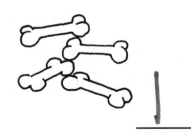 1

If you take away 0 bones from Sam how many will be left?

g 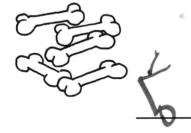 5

h 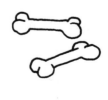 2

i 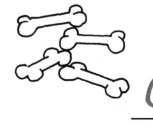 4

Look at the signs we can use in place of words ...

 **take away 2** is

3   –   2 =   1

QUICK TIP!
– means
take away

2.   Write the answers.

a   – 2 = __1__   **b**  – 1 = _____

c 4 – 2 = _____   **d** 5 – 3 = _____

e 2 – 2 = _____   **f** 3 – 1 = _____

How did I do?   Total
                                      /14

More practice? Go to www

Challenge yourself

Write the answers.

a 5 take away 3 is _____ .

b Sam has 4 bones. He hides 1.
    How many bones does Sam have left? _____

c How many less than 5 is 4? _____

d 3 taken from a number leaves 1.
    What is the number? _____

Addition facts to 5

Look at how many ways I can make 4.

$$0 + 4$$
$$1 + 3$$
$$2 + 2 \qquad = \qquad 4$$
$$3 + 1$$
$$4 + 0$$

1. **Show all the different ways you can make 3.**

   $0 + 3 = 3$

   $1 + \underline{\qquad} = 3$

   $2 + \underline{\qquad} = 3$

   $\underline{\qquad} + 0 = 3$

2. **Show all the different ways you can make 5.**

   $\underline{\qquad} + 5 = 5$ $\qquad\qquad$ $\underline{\qquad} + \underline{\qquad} = 5$

   $\underline{\qquad} + 4 = 5$ $\qquad\qquad$ $\underline{\qquad} + \underline{\qquad} = 5$

   $\underline{\qquad} + 3 = 5$ $\qquad\qquad$ $\underline{\qquad} + \underline{\qquad} = 5$

3. **Show all the different ways you can make 2.**

   $\underline{\qquad} + \underline{\qquad} = 2$

   $\underline{\qquad} + \underline{\qquad} = 2$

   $\underline{\qquad} + \underline{\qquad} = 2$

4. **Write the answers.**

$$0 + 0 = 0$$

$1 + 1 = \underline{\quad}$

$2 + 2 = \underline{\quad}$

Look, the answer goes up **2** each time.

5. **Check the answers.** ✓ = correct   ✗ = wrong

a $2 + 3 = 4$ ✗

b $3 + 1 = 5$

c $3 + 1 = 4$

d $2 + 2 = 4$

e $2 + 1 = 3$

f $5 + 0 = 5$

g $3 + 2 = 3$

h $2 + 1 = 4$

How did I do?

Total
/21

More practice? Go to www

Challenge yourself

0   **1**   **2**   **3**

Choose two of these numbers at a time. Add them together.
Find all the different totals that can be made.

____ ____ ____ ____ ____

9

2D shapes

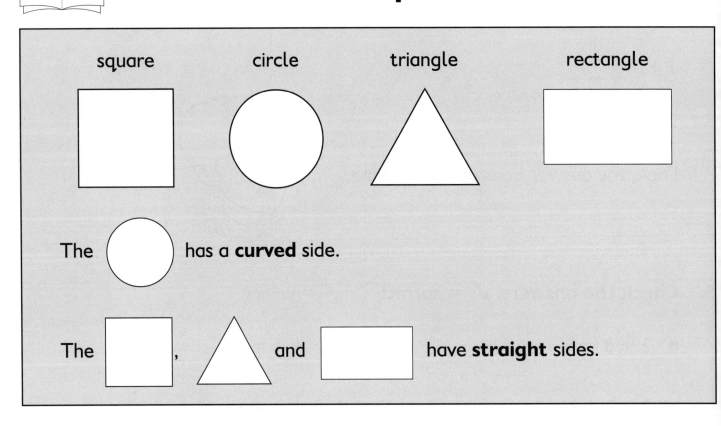

square   circle   triangle   rectangle

The ◯ has a **curved** side.

The ☐, △ and ▭ have **straight** sides.

1. **Draw over these shapes. Answer the questions.**

    a How many sides?

    _____ sides

    b How many sides?

    _____ sides

2. **Colour the shapes.**

    a 4 corners – blue   **b** 3 corners – green   **c** no corners – yellow

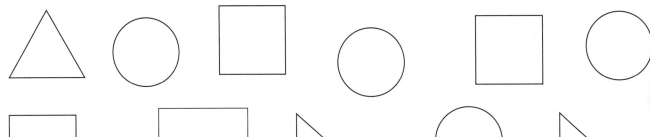
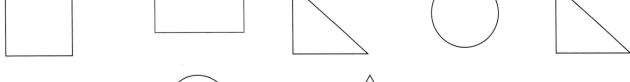

10

3. In each box draw a ...

square

triangle

circle

rectangle

4. Draw the missing shape in the gap.

a A _____ has 3 sides.

b A _____, _____ and a _____ have straight sides.

c A _____ and a _____ have 4 sides.

How did I do?

Total

/12

More practice? Go to www

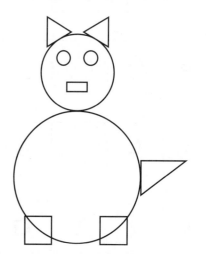

Patterns

A **pattern** can happen again and again, like this ...

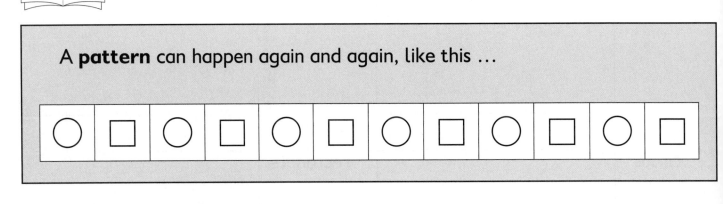

1. Finish these patterns.

a | X | ◯ | X | ◯ | X | | | | | | |

b | A | B | A | B | A | | | | | | |

c | ● | ◯ | ● | ◯ | | | | | | | |

d | ☺ | ☹ | ☺ | ☹ | | | | | | |

2. Fill in the gaps.

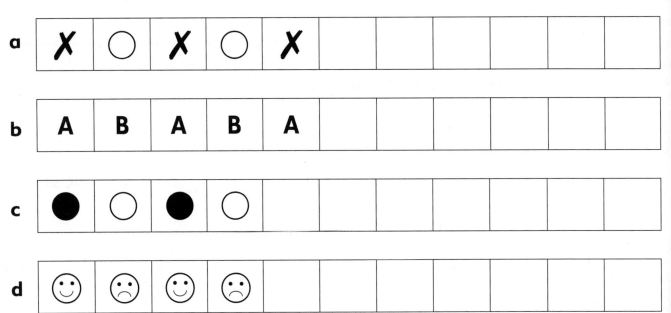

a | ✓ | X | | X | | X | ✓ | X | | |

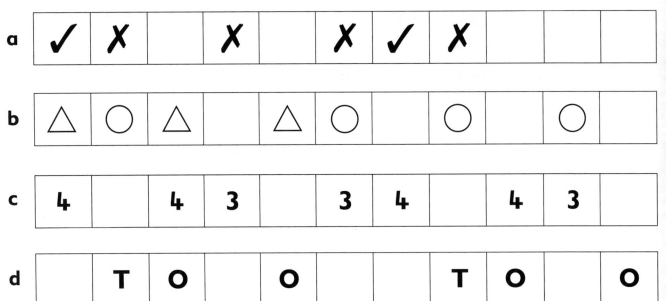

b | △ | ◯ | △ | | △ | ◯ | | ◯ | | ◯ | |

c | 4 | | 4 | 3 | | 3 | 4 | | 4 | 3 |

d | | T | O | | O | | | T | O | | O |

12

Look carefully at this pattern.
This time the pattern uses **4 shapes**.

| △ | □ | ○ | ○ | △ | □ | ○ | ○ | △ | □ | ○ |

3. **Now try these. Look carefully at each pattern.**

a | ✗ | ✓ | ○ | ✗ | ✓ | ○ | | | | | |

b | **A** | **A** | **B** | **B** | **A** | | | | | | |

c | **2** | **4** | **4** | **2** | **4** | | | | | | |

d | △ | △ | ▽ | ▽ | ▽ | △ | | | | | |

e | ○ | ● | ○ | ○ | ● | | | | | | |

How did I do?

Total
13

More practice? Go to **www**

Challenge yourself

Make some patterns of your own.

a Use △ and □.

| | | | | | | | | | | |

b Use ✓ and ✗.

| | | | | | | | | | | |

13

Comparing measures

The train is **longer** than the car.

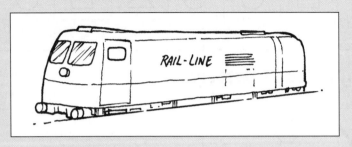

1. Colour in the longer object.

a

b
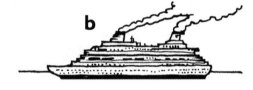

c

Bob is **taller** than Tom.

Bob  Tom

2. Tick the taller child.

a

_____ _____

b

_____ _____

c

_____ _____

The dog is **heavier** than the bird.

3. Colour in the heavier animal.

a
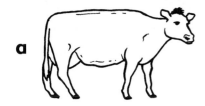

b

c

How did I do?

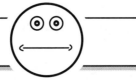

Total

/9

More practice? Go to www

Challenge yourself

One cup of juice filled the jug this much.
How many cups of juice do you think would
be needed to fill the whole jug?

15

Time – days and seasons

Time is measured in **units**.
Here are some units that measure **time**.

minutes   hours   days   weeks   months   seasons

1. **Put the pictures in the right order.**

1 _I get up._

2 _____

3 _____

4 _____

5 _____

I go to bed.

I go home.

I get up.

I go to school.

I get dressed.

2. Put the days of the week in order.

Tuesday Sunday Wednesday Saturday

Friday Thursday Monday

1 Sunday _____   2 _____

3 Tuesday _____   4 _____

5 Thursday _____ 6 _____

7 _____

3. Answer these questions.

| Spring | Summer | Autumn | Winter |

a In which season do bulbs begin to grow? _____

b In which season can you kick leaves on the ground? _____

How did I do?   Total

                                                          /10

More practice? Go to www

Challenge yourself

In a week how many times do you...

a ...go to school? ☐   b ...have breakfast? ☐

c ...clean your teeth? ☐   d ...go to bed? ☐

How am I doing?

1. **a** Colour 3 apples.

    b How many apples?  _____

2. **Fill in the missing number.**

    a 1 2 3 [   ] 5   **b** 2 [   ] 4

3. **Write the answers.**

    a 3 + 2 = _____   **b** 2 + 1 = _____

    c 5 − 2 = _____   **d** 3 − 2 = _____

4. **How many different ways can you make 3?**

    _____ + _____ = 3   _____ + _____ = 3

    _____ + _____ = 3   _____ + _____ = 3

5. **a** Draw a square in the box.   **b** Draw a triangle in the box.
        Write how many sides.   Write how many sides.

_____ sides   _____ sides

6. Finish the patterns.

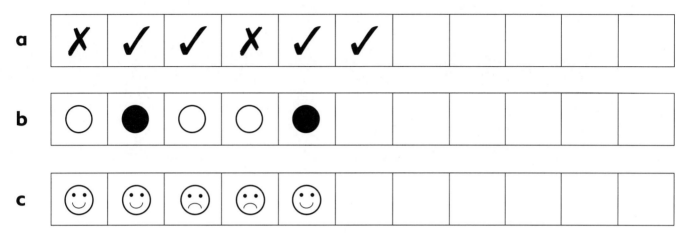

a ✗ ✓ ✓ ✗ ✓ ✓

b ○ ● ○ ○ ●

c ☺ ☺ ☹ ☹ ☺

7. Which do you think is the tallest?

Draw a circle around the answer.

a door   **a cup**   **a giraffe**   **a book**

8. Which do you think is the heaviest?

Draw a circle around the answer.

a cat   **a pig**   **a horse**

9. Which day comes after...

a Tuesday? _____

b Friday? _____

c Sunday? _____

Total

 /22

More practice? Go to www

Numbers to 10

Look at the numbers. They go up in **order**.

1 2 3 4 5 6 7 8 9 10

1. **a** Colour 6 flowers.

   b Colour 8 flowers.

   c Colour 2 flowers.

2. **Draw the flowers.**

   a 5 flowers   **b** 8 flowers   **c** 6 flowers

3. **How many flowers?**

   a  _____

   b  _____

   c  _____

   d  _____

4. **Join the dots to make the shapes. Start on 1 each time. Use a ruler.**

a
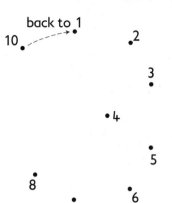

b
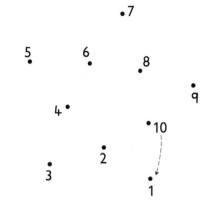

c
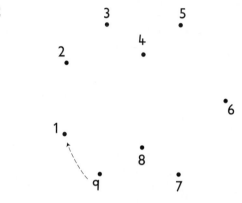

d

5. **Which number comes first when you count in order?**

a 7 or 6? _6_

b 4 or 5? _____

c 5 or 6? _____

How did I do?

Total
/16

More practice? Go to www

Challenge yourself

Look at the number line.

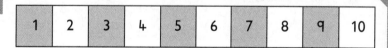

| 1 | 2 | 3 | 4 | 5 | 6 | 7 | 8 | 9 | 10 |

a Which number comes before 7? _____

b Which number comes after 5? _____

c Which number comes after 9? _____

d Which number comes before 2? _____

Addition to 10

Remember, we can **add** numbers together like this …

 and  makes

5   and   2   makes   7

These are the **signs** we can use in place of words.

5 + 2 = 7

1. **Write the missing numbers.**

   a  and  makes _____

   b  and  makes _____

   c  +  = _____

   d  +  = _____

2. **Write the numbers in the gaps.**

   a  and  makes

   6   +   4   =   10

b  and  makes

_____ + _____ = _____

c  and  makes

_____ + _____ = _____

d  and  makes

_____ + _____ = _____

3. Add the numbers.

a 6 + 2 = _____   **b** 8 + 1 = _____

c 4 + 5 = _____   **d** 6 + 4 = _____

e 7 + 3 = _____   **f** 7 + 1 = _____

How did I do?      Total

13

More practice? Go to www

Challenge yourself

a What is the sum of 3 and 4? _____

b What must I add to 7 to make 10? _____

c How many are 2 and 6 altogether? _____

d What is my number if I add 4 to it to make 9? _____

Subtraction to 10

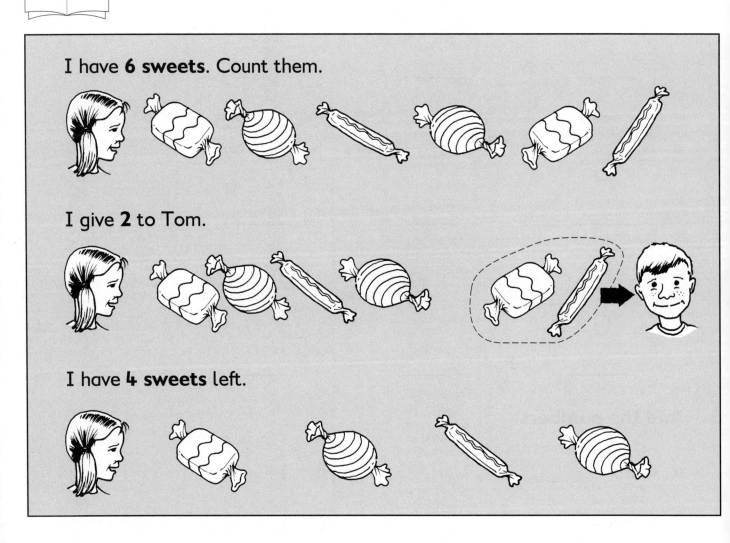

I have **6 sweets**. Count them.

I give **2** to Tom.

I have **4 sweets** left.

1. **If you take away 2 sweets from each bag how many will you have left?**

a _____ *1*

b  _____

c _____

d  _____

e  _____

f _____

Now take away 5 sweets.

g  _____

h _____

i _____

24

Look at the signs we can use in place of words...

 take away 3   is

7   −   3   =   4

QUICK TIP!
− means
take away

2. Write the answers.

a − 2 = _____

b − 5 = _____

c − 4 = _____

d − 6 = _____

3. Write the answers.

a 6 − 2 = _____   b 8 − 6 = _____   c 3 − 1 = _____

d 8 − 4 = _____   e 9 − 5 = _____   f 10 − 4 = _____

How did I do?   

Total

/18

More practice? Go to www

Challenge yourself

What is the answer?

a 5 less than 9 is _____ .

b If you had 7 pens but lost 3 how many would you have left? _____

c What number must I take from 6 to leave 0? _____

d Jay had 10 sweets. He ate 6. How many did he have left? _____

Knowing when to add or subtract to 10

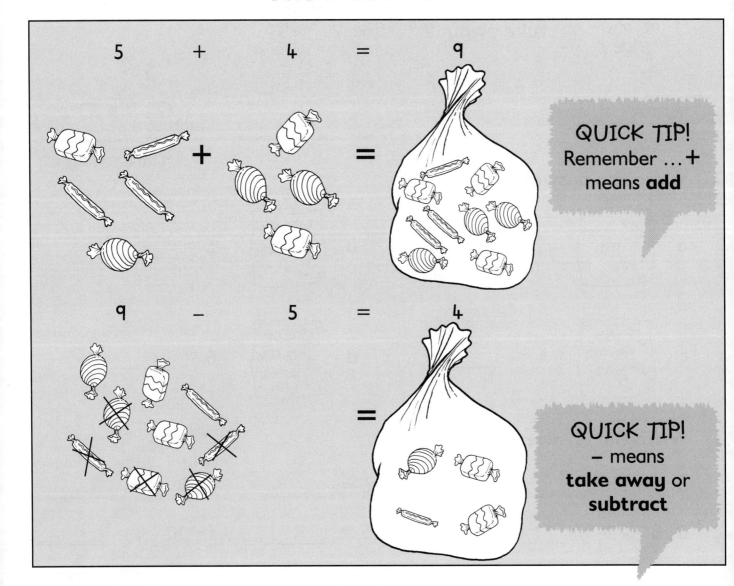

5   +   4   =   9

+   =

QUICK TIP!
Remember ... +
means **add**

9   –   5   =   4

=

QUICK TIP!
– means
take away or
subtract

1. **Answer these.**

   a 6 + 2 = _____   b 9 – 3 = _____

   c 7 – 3 = _____   d 8 + 2 = _____

   e 5 + 4 = _____   f 8 – 2 = _____

2. **Which sign, + or – ? Fill in the gaps.**

   a 6 $\boxed{+}$ 3 = 9   b 9 $\boxed{}$ 6 = 3

   c 5 $\boxed{}$ 5 = 10   d 7 $\boxed{}$ 2 = 9

   e 5 $\boxed{}$ 3 = 8   f 7 $\boxed{}$ 2 = 5

3. **Which sign should you use?**

Fill in the gaps with + or −.

a 6 less 3 = 3

    6 | − | 3 = 3

b 5 subtract 4 = 1

    5 | | 4 = 1

c 8 and 2 more = 10

    8 | | 2 = 10

d 2 add 7 = 9

    2 | | 7 = 9

e 9 take away 7 = 2

    9 | | 7 = 2

f 7 less 3 = 4

    7 | | 3 = 4

g 10 subtract 6 = 4

    10 | | 6 = 4

h 1 and 3 more = 4

    1 | | 3 = 4

How did I do?

Total
/18

More practice? Go to **www**

Challenge yourself

Write the correct sign in the gap. + or −?

a 10p   8p = 2p

b 7p   2p = 9p

c 8p   5p = 3p

d 2p   6p = 8p

e 9p   4p = 5p

Addition facts to 10

Look at how many ways we can make 7.

0 + 7 = 7	4 + 3 = 7
1 + 6 = 7	5 + 2 = 7
2 + 5 = 7	6 + 1 = 7
3 + 4 = 7	7 + 0 = 7

1. **How many different ways can you make 9?**

0 + 9 = 9   5 + _____ = 9

1 + _____ = 9   6 + 3 = _____

_____ + 7 = 9   _____ + 2 = 9

3 + 6 = _____   8 + _____ = 9

_____ + 5 = 9   _____ + 0 = 9

2. **How many different ways can you make 4?**
   Write them in the box.

3. **Fill in the gaps.**

0 + 0 = __0__   1 + 1 = _____

2 + 2 = _____   3 + 3 = _____

4 + 4 = _____   5 + 5 = _____

How many does the answer go up by each time? _____

4. **Check the answers.** ✓ = correct   ✗ = wrong

a 6 + 3 = 9 [✓]

b 7 − 3 = 5 [✗]

c 2 + 7 = 10 [✗]

d 5 + 3 = 8 [✓]

e 5 + 5 = 9 [ ]

f 7 − 4 = 3 [✓]

How did I do?

Total

22

More practice? Go to www

Challenge yourself

Answer these questions.

a There were 8 buttons on a coat.
3 fell off. How many were left? _____

b 5 apples were on the tree. 2 fell off.
How many were left? _____

c There were 10 cakes. 3 were eaten.
How many were left? _____

d A bag of 7 sweets had a hole in it.
4 sweets fell out. How many were left? _____

Doubles and halves

Here is a bag of 4 sweets.

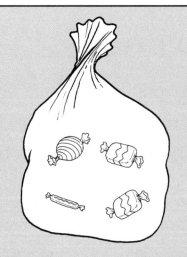

QUICK TIP!
double = 2 of the
same number

QUICK TIP!
half = a number
split into 2

If we **double** the number of sweets we get 8.

If we **halve** the number of sweets we get 2.

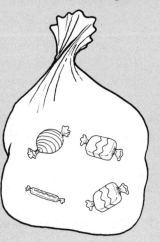

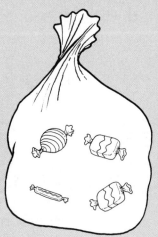

1. **Draw a line to the answer.**

   a $1 + 1 =$ 6

   b $2 + 2 =$ 8

   c $3 + 3 =$ 4

   d $4 + 4 =$ 10

   e $5 + 5 =$ 2

2. **What are**

   a 2 lots of 5? _____

   b 2 lots of 4? _____

   c 2 lots of 3? _____

   d 2 lots of 2? _____

3. **Halve the sweets in each bag. How many are left?**

a 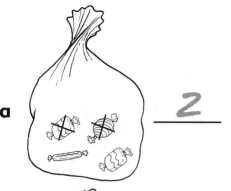 _2_

b 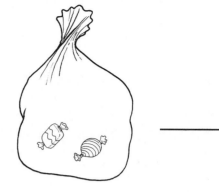 _____

c 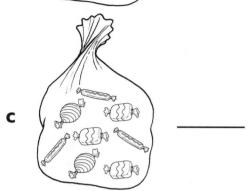 _____

d 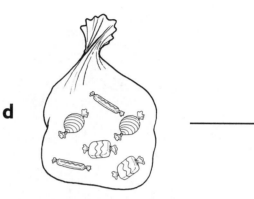 _____

4. **Write the answer. Draw pictures to help if you need to.**

a Half of 10 __5__   b Half of 8 _____   c Half of 6 _____

How did I do?			

Total
/13

More practice? Go to   www

Challenge yourself

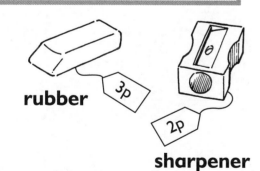

rubber   3p

2p
sharpener

5p **pad**

4p **pencil**

How much are

a 2 pencils? _____   b 2 rubbers? _____

c 2 sharpeners? _____   d 2 pads? _____

First or last, more or less

When something comes **first** it is at the **beginning**.

When something comes **last** it is at the **end**.

1. **Look at the picture. Answer the questions.**

   a Which snail is last? _____

   b Which snail is 2nd? _____

   c Which snail is 8th? _____

   d Which snail is first? _____

   e Which snail is 5th? _____

No Nonsense
Maths

5-6 years

Parents notes

What your child will learn from this book

Bond No Nonsense will help your child to understand and become more confident in their maths work. This book features all the main maths objectives covered by your child's class teacher during the school year. It provides clear, straightforward teaching and learning of the essentials in a rigorous, step-by-step way.

How you can help

Following a few simple guidelines will ensure that your child gets the best from this book:

- Explain that the book will help your child become confident in their maths work.
- If your child has difficulty reading the text on the page or understanding a question, do provide help.
- Provide scrap paper to give your child extra space for rough working.
- Encourage your child to complete all the exercises in a lesson. You can mark the work using this answer section (which you will also find on the website). Your child can record their own impressions of the work using the 'How did I do' feature.

How did I do?

- The 'How am I doing?' sections provide a further review of progress.

Using the website – www.bondlearning.co.uk

- The website provides extra practice of every skill in the book. So if your child does not feel confident about a lesson, they can go to the website and have another go.
- For every page of this book you will find further practice questions and their answers available to download.
- To access the extra practice pages:
  1. Go to www.bondlearning.co.uk
  2. Click on 'Maths'.
  3. Click on '5-6 years'.
  4. Click on the lesson you want.

Bond No Nonsense 5-6 years Answers

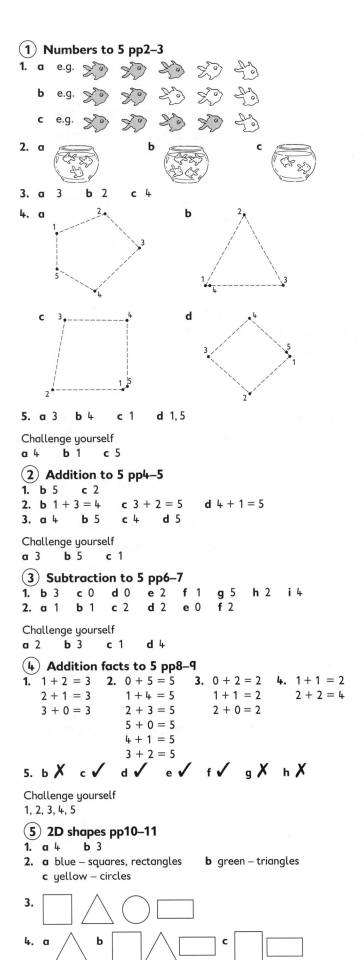

(1) Numbers to 5 pp2–3

1. a e.g.

 b e.g.

 c e.g.

2. a   b   c

3. a 3   b 2   c 4

4. a   b

 c   d

5. a 3   b 4   c 1   d 1, 5

Challenge yourself
a 4   b 1   c 5

(2) Addition to 5 pp4–5

1. b 5   c 2
2. b 1 + 3 = 4   c 3 + 2 = 5   d 4 + 1 = 5
3. a 4   b 5   c 4   d 5

Challenge yourself
a 3   b 5   c 1

(3) Subtraction to 5 pp6–7

1. b 3   c 0   d 0   e 2   f 1   g 5   h 2   i 4
2. a 1   b 1   c 2   d 2   e 0   f 2

Challenge yourself
a 2   b 3   c 1   d 4

(4) Addition facts to 5 pp8–9

1. $1 + 2 = 3$ **2.** $0 + 5 = 5$ **3.** $0 + 2 = 2$ **4.** $1 + 1 = 2$
$2 + 1 = 3$ $1 + 4 = 5$ $1 + 1 = 2$ $2 + 2 = 4$
$3 + 0 = 3$ $2 + 3 = 5$ $2 + 0 = 2$
             $5 + 0 = 5$
             $4 + 1 = 5$
             $3 + 2 = 5$

5. b ✗   c ✓   d ✓   e ✓   f ✓   g ✗   h ✗

Challenge yourself
1, 2, 3, 4, 5

(5) 2D shapes pp10–11

1. a 4   b 3
2. a blue – squares, rectangles   b green – triangles
   c yellow – circles

3.

4. a   b   c

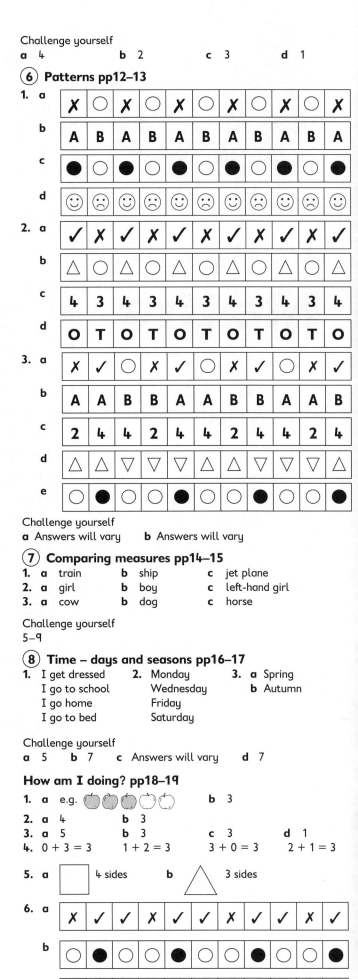

Challenge yourself
a 4   b 2   c 3   d 1

(6) Patterns pp12–13

1. a ✗ ○ ✗ ○ ✗ ○ ✗ ○ ✗ ○ ✗
 b A B A B A B A B A B A
 c ● ○ ● ○ ● ○ ● ○ ● ○ ●
 d ☺ ☹ ☺ ☹ ☺ ☹ ☺ ☹ ☺ ☹ ☺

2. a ✓ ✗ ✓ ✗ ✓ ✗ ✓ ✗ ✓ ✗ ✓
 b △ ○ △ ○ △ ○ △ ○ △ ○ △
 c 4 3 4 3 4 3 4 3 4 3 4
 d O T O T O T O T O T O

3. a ✗ ✓ ○ ✗ ✓ ○ ✗ ✓ ○ ✗ ✓
 b A A B B A A B B A A B
 c 2 4 4 2 4 4 2 4 4 2 4
 d △ △ ▽ ▽ ▽ △ △ ▽ ▽ ▽ △
 e ○ ● ○ ○ ● ○ ○ ● ○ ○ ●

Challenge yourself
a Answers will vary   b Answers will vary

(7) Comparing measures pp14–15

1. a train   b ship   c jet plane
2. a girl   b boy   c left-hand girl
3. a cow   b dog   c horse

Challenge yourself
5–9

(8) Time – days and seasons pp16–17

1. I get dressed   **2.** Monday   **3.** a Spring
 I go to school   Wednesday   b Autumn
 I go home   Friday
 I go to bed   Saturday

Challenge yourself
a 5   b 7   c Answers will vary   d 7

How am I doing? pp18–19

1. a e.g.   b 3
2. a 4   b 3
3. a 5   b 3   c 3   d 1
4. $0 + 3 = 3$ $1 + 2 = 3$ $3 + 0 = 3$ $2 + 1 = 3$

5. a ☐ 4 sides   b △ 3 sides

6. a ✗ ✓ ✓ ✗ ✓ ✓ ✗ ✓ ✓ ✗ ✓
 b ○ ● ○ ○ ● ○ ○ ● ○ ○ ●
 c ☺ ☺ ☹ ☹ ☺ ☹ ☺ ☹ ☺ ☹

A2

7. a giraffe

8. a horse

9. a Wednesday   b Saturday   c Monday

⑨ **Numbers to 10 pp20–21**

1. a e.g.

    b e.g.

    c e.g.

2. a   b   c

3. a 7   b 5   c 8   d 10

4. a   b

    c   d

5. b 4   c 5

Challenge yourself

a 6   b 6   c 10   d 1

⑩ **Addition to 10 pp22–23**

1. a 9   b 8   c 6   d 8

2. b $3 + 5 = 8$ c $4 + 2 = 6$ d $6 + 3 = 9$

3. a 8   b 9   c 9   d 10   e 10   f 8

Challenge yourself

a 7   b 3   c 8   d 5

⑪ **Subtraction to 10 pp24–25**

1. b 3   c 6   d 2   e 7   f 0   g 1   h 5   i 2

2. a 2   b 0   c 3   d 2

3. a 4   b 2   c 2   d 4   e 4   f 6

Challenge yourself

a 4   b 4   c 6   d 4

⑫ **Knowing when to add or subtract to 10 pp26–27**

1. a 8   b 6   c 4   d 10   e 9   f 6

2. b –   c +   d +   e +   f –

3. b –   c +   d +   e –   f –   g –   h +

Challenge yourself

a –   b +   c –   d +   e –

⑬ **Addition facts to 10 pp28–29**

1.

$0 + 9 = 9$	$5 + 4 = 9$	$1 + 8 = 9$
$6 + 3 = 9$	$2 + 7 = 9$	$7 + 2 = 9$
$3 + 6 = 9$	$8 + 1 = 9$	$4 + 5 = 9$
$9 + 0 = 9$		

2.

$0 + 4 = 4$	$1 + 3 = 4$	$2 + 2 = 4$
$3 + 1 = 4$	$4 + 0 = 4$	

3.

$0 + 0 = 0$	$1 + 1 = 2$	$2 + 2 = 4$
$3 + 3 = 6$	$4 + 4 = 8$	$5 + 5 = 10$

    Answer goes up by 2 each time.

4. a ✓   b ✗   c ✗   d ✓   e ✗   f ✓

Challenge yourself

a 5   b 3   c 7   d 3

⑭ **Doubles and halves pp30–31**

1. b $2 + 2 = 4$ c $3 + 3 = 6$

    d $4 + 4 = 8$ e $5 + 5 = 10$

2. a 10   b 8   c 6   d 4

3. b 1   c 4   d 3

4. b 4   c 3

Challenge yourself

a 8p   b 6p   c 4p   d 10p

⑮ **First or last, more or less pp32–33**

1. a j   b b   c h   d a   e e

2. a 9   b 7   c 5   d 4   e 9   f 3   g 9   h 6

Challenge yourself

d 🌙   e ◇   f ▭

⑯ **3D shapes pp34–35**

1. a   blue – cylinder, cone, sphere   b 3

    c   circled – cube, cuboid, cylinder, cone   d   cube, cuboid

2. a   sphere   b   cuboid   c   cuboid

Challenge yourself

baked bean tin – cylinder   ice-cream cone – cone

tennis ball – sphere   packet of biscuits – cylinder

toy box – cube   shoe box – cuboid

⑰ **Time – o'clock pp36–37**

1. a   5 o'clock   b   9 o'clock

    c   1 o'clock   d   7 o'clock

2. a   b   c

    d   e   f

Challenge yourself

a 5 o'clock   b 1 o'clock   c 2 hours

⑱ **Solving problems pp38–39**

1. a 10   b 9   c 4

2. a Answers will vary   b Answers will vary

Challenge yourself

4 ways, (plus 9 using rearranged order):

1, 1, 5	(1, 5, 1 or 5, 1, 1)
1, 2, 4	(1, 4, 2 or 4, 2, 1 or 4, 1, 2 or 2, 1, 4 or 2, 4, 1)
1, 3, 3	(3, 1, 3 or 3, 3, 1)
2, 2, 3	(2, 3, 2 or 3, 2, 2)

How am I doing? pp40–41

1. a 7   b 10

2. a 9   b 10   c 6   d 6

3. a 4   b 1

4. a +   b –

5. a 0   b 6   c 2   d 8   e 4   f 10

6. a 4   b 10   c 1   d 6

7. a 7   b 4

8. sphere

9. 7 o'clock

10. 10

⑲ **Reading and writing numbers to 20 pp42–43**

1. a   b   c

2. a 13   b 16   c 10   d 19

3. a 18 – circled in red (5 times)   b 17 – circled in green (3 times)

    c 20 – circled in blue (4 times)

4. a 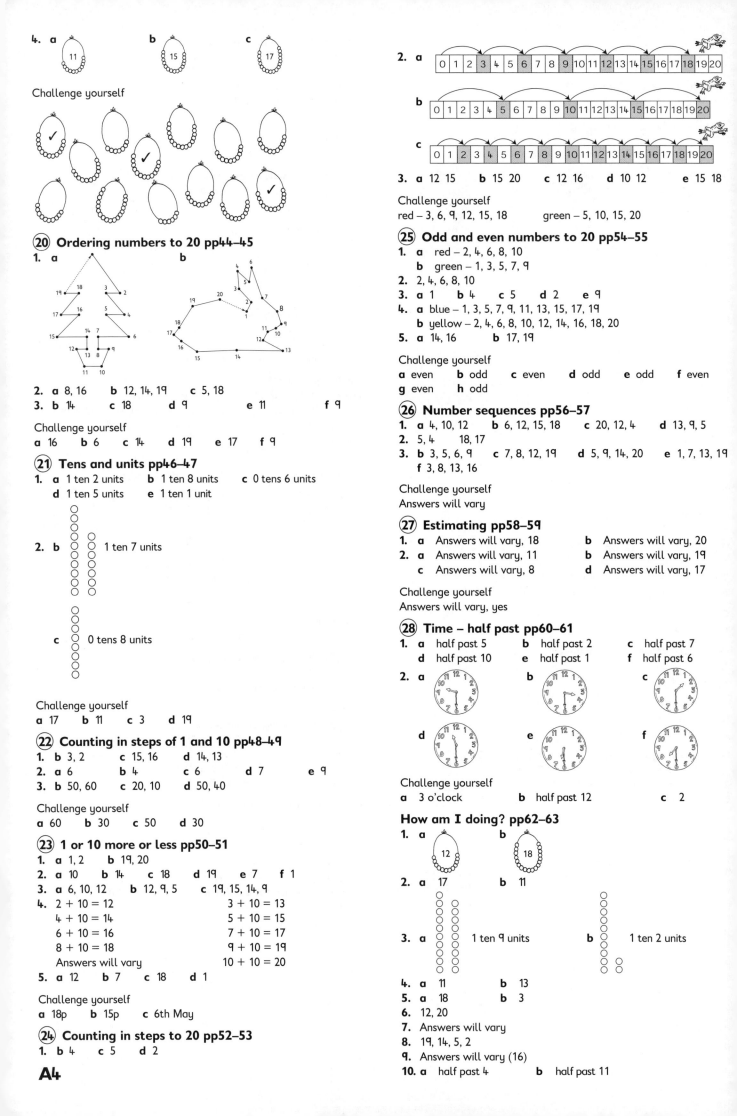 11   **b** 15   **c** 17

Challenge yourself

20 Ordering numbers to 20 pp44–45

1. a   **b**

2. a 8, 16   **b** 12, 14, 19   **c** 5, 18
3. b 14   **c** 18   **d** 9   **e** 11   **f** 9

Challenge yourself
a 16   **b** 6   **c** 14   **d** 19   **e** 17   **f** 9

21 Tens and units pp46–47

1. a 1 ten 2 units   **b** 1 ten 8 units   **c** 0 tens 6 units
   d 1 ten 5 units   **e** 1 ten 1 unit

2. b 1 ten 7 units

   c 0 tens 8 units

Challenge yourself
a 17   **b** 11   **c** 3   **d** 19

22 Counting in steps of 1 and 10 pp48–49

1. b 3, 2   **c** 15, 16   **d** 14, 13
2. a 6   **b** 4   **c** 6   **d** 7   **e** 9
3. b 50, 60   **c** 20, 10   **d** 50, 40

Challenge yourself
a 60   **b** 30   **c** 50   **d** 30

23 1 or 10 more or less pp50–51

1. a 1, 2   **b** 19, 20
2. a 10   **b** 14   **c** 18   **d** 19   **e** 7   **f** 1
3. a 6, 10, 12   **b** 12, 9, 5   **c** 19, 15, 14, 9
4. 2 + 10 = 12   3 + 10 = 13
    4 + 10 = 14   5 + 10 = 15
    6 + 10 = 16   7 + 10 = 17
    8 + 10 = 18   9 + 10 = 19
    Answers will vary   10 + 10 = 20
5. a 12   **b** 7   **c** 18   **d** 1

Challenge yourself
a 18p   **b** 15p   **c** 6th May

24 Counting in steps to 20 pp52–53

1. b 4   **c** 5   **d** 2

A4

---

2. a

   b

   c

3. a 12 15   **b** 15 20   **c** 12 16   **d** 10 12   **e** 15 18

Challenge yourself
red – 3, 6, 9, 12, 15, 18   green – 5, 10, 15, 20

25 Odd and even numbers to 20 pp54–55

1. a red – 2, 4, 6, 8, 10
   b green – 1, 3, 5, 7, 9
2. 2, 4, 6, 8, 10
3. a 1   **b** 4   **c** 5   **d** 2   **e** 9
4. a blue – 1, 3, 5, 7, 9, 11, 13, 15, 17, 19
   b yellow – 2, 4, 6, 8, 10, 12, 14, 16, 18, 20
5. a 14, 16   **b** 17, 19

Challenge yourself
a even   **b** odd   **c** even   **d** odd   **e** odd   **f** even
g even   **h** odd

26 Number sequences pp56–57

1. a 4, 10, 12   **b** 6, 12, 15, 18   **c** 20, 12, 4   **d** 13, 9, 5
2. 5, 4   18, 17
3. b 3, 5, 6, 9   **c** 7, 8, 12, 19   **d** 5, 9, 14, 20   **e** 1, 7, 13, 19
   f 3, 8, 13, 16

Challenge yourself
Answers will vary

27 Estimating pp58–59

1. a Answers will vary, 18   **b** Answers will vary, 20
2. a Answers will vary, 11   **b** Answers will vary, 19
   c Answers will vary, 8   **d** Answers will vary, 17

Challenge yourself
Answers will vary, yes

28 Time – half past pp60–61

1. a half past 5   **b** half past 2   **c** half past 7
   d half past 10   **e** half past 1   **f** half past 6
2. a   **b**   **c**

   d   **e**   **f**

Challenge yourself
a 3 o'clock   **b** half past 12   **c** 2

How am I doing? pp62–63

1. a   **b**
   12   18

2. a 17   **b** 11

3. a 1 ten 9 units   **b** 1 ten 2 units

4. a 11   **b** 13
5. a 18   **b** 3
6. 12, 20
7. Answers will vary
8. 19, 14, 5, 2
9. Answers will vary (16)
10. a half past 4   **b** half past 11

2. **Answer the questions.**

a Which is more... 5 or 9? _____   **b** Which is less... 7 or 10? _____

c Which is more... 5 or 1? _____   **d** Which is less... 6 or 4? _____

e Which is more... 2 or 9? _____   **f** Which is less... 8 or 3? _____

g Which is more... 9 or 3? _____   **h** Which is less... 7 or 6? _____

Total

| How did I do? |  | |  |

 13

More practice? Go to

Challenge yourself

Fill in the gaps with shapes. Put them where they need to go.

a Put a △ first.

b Put a ▢ in 6th place.

c Put a ○ last.

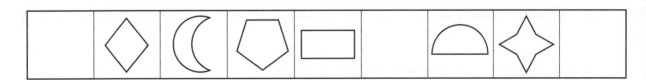

Now answer these questions. Draw the shapes.

d Which shape is 3rd? _____

e Which shape is 8th? _____

f Which shape comes after this shape? 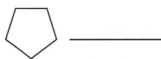 _____

3D shapes

These are all **3D shapes**.

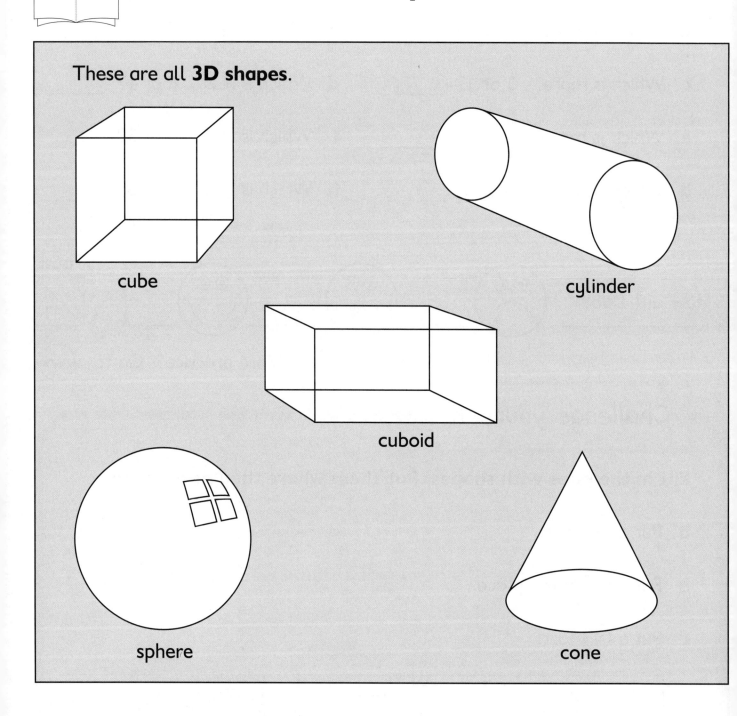

cube

cylinder

cuboid

sphere

cone

1. **a** Colour blue the shapes that can roll.

    b How many shapes have one or more corners? _____

    c Put a circle around each shape with flat faces.

    d Which 2 shapes have the same number of faces and corners?

    _____   _____

2. Look at these shapes.

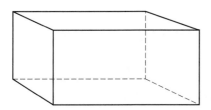 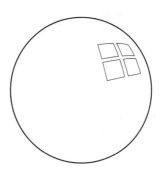

Write the name of the shape in the gaps.

a The _____ can roll.

b The _____ has corners.

c The _____ has flat faces.

How did I do?

Total

8

More practice? Go to **www**

Challenge yourself

With a line, match the item with the shape words.

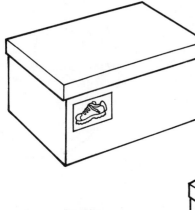  

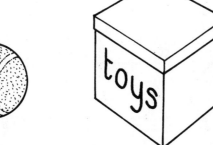 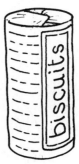

cube   sphere   cone   cuboid   cylinder

Time – o'clock

We know what **time** it is by looking at a clock.

This clock shows it is 3 o'clock.

The **big hand** is pointing at the 12.

The **small hand** is pointing at the 3.

1. **What is the time?**

a ____ o'clock    b ____ o'clock

c ____ o'clock    d ____ o'clock

2. Draw the small hand on the clocks.

a 3 o'clock

b 5 o'clock

c 9 o'clock

d 11 o'clock

e 7 o'clock

f 1 o'clock

How did I do?

Total
/10

More practice? Go to www

Challenge yourself

It is 4 o'clock.

a What time will it be in one hour's time? _____

b What time was it 3 hours ago? _____

c In how many hours will it be 6 o'clock? _____

Solving Problems

When you try and solve a problem you are looking for an **answer**.

Sometimes there is more than one answer!

1. **Find the answers to these problems.**

   a Tom has 5 more sweets than Alijah.
   Alijah has 5 sweets. How many sweets does Tom have?

   _____

   b Ross is 3 years older than Alice. Alice is 6 years old.
   How old is Ross?

   _____

   c Meena has 12 pets. Dan has 8 fewer pets than Meena.
   How many pets does Dan have?

   _____

2. Solve these number puzzles.
Use the numbers 0–9.

a Put a number in each circle so each side of the triangle adds up to 10.

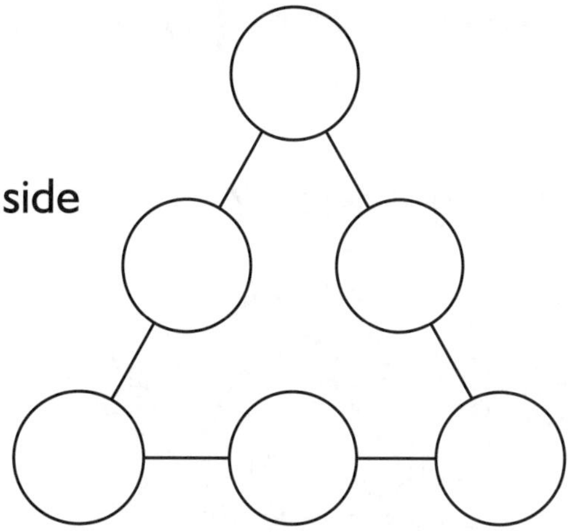

b Put a number in each circle so each side of the triangle adds up to 9.

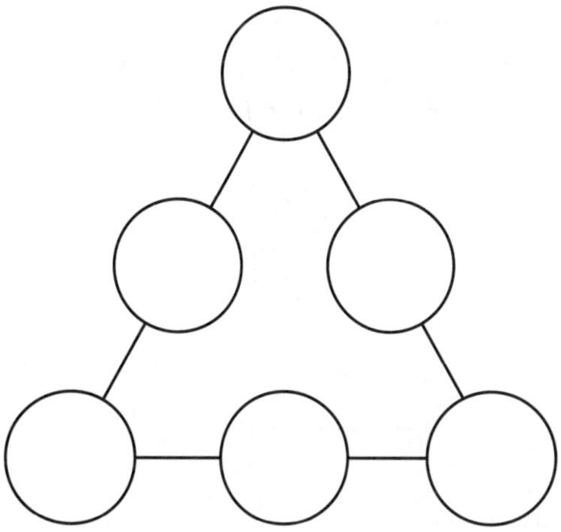

Total

/5

More practice? Go to www

Challenge yourself

How many different ways can you put 7 conkers in 3 boxes?
You must have at least one conker in each box.

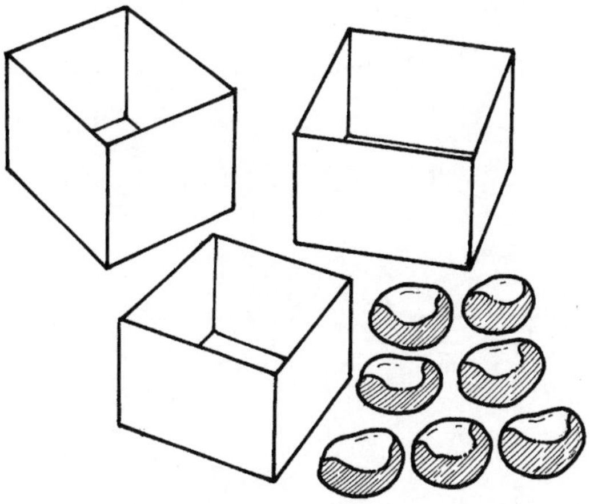

How am I doing?

1. **How many flowers?**

a  _____

b 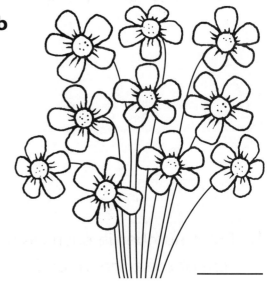 _____

2. **a** $6 + 3 =$ _____   **b** $5 + 5 =$ _____

   c $5 + 1 =$ _____   **d** $6 + 0 =$ _____

3. **Take away 4 sweets from each bag.**

a 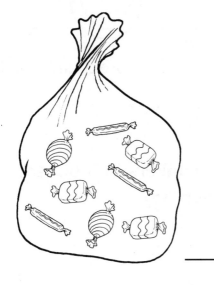 _____

b  _____

4. **Which sign is missing? Fill in the gaps.**

   a 5 _____ $3 = 8$ **b** 5 _____ $2 = 3$

5. Fill in the gaps.

   a $0 + 0 =$ _____   **b** $3 + 3 =$ _____

   c $1 + 1 =$ _____   **d** $4 + 4 =$ _____

   e $2 + 2 =$ _____   **f** $5 + 5 =$ _____

6. Write the answer.

   a Half of 8 _____   **b** Double 5 _____

   c Half of 2 _____   **d** Double 3 _____

7. **a** Which number comes before 8? _____

   b Which number comes after 3? _____

8. Which can you roll, a sphere or a cube 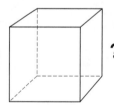 ?

_____

9. What is the time?  _____ o'clock

10. Shannon has collected 8 conkers.
Josh has collected 2 conkers more than Shannon.
How many conkers has Josh collected?

_____

Reading and writing numbers to 20

Look at the numbers.
They go from **1 to 20**.

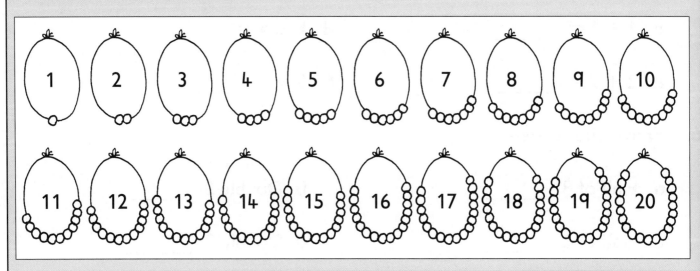

1. Colour

a 9 beads red.

b 12 beads green.

c 17 beads blue.

2. How many beads are on each necklace?

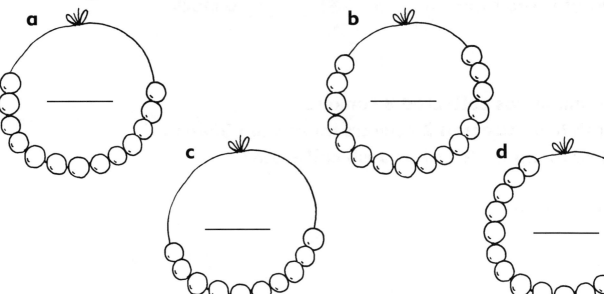

a

b

c

d

3. **a** Put a red circle around each number 18.
   b Put a green circle around each number 17.
   c Put a blue circle around each number 20.

   12   18   17   5   20   18   17

   8   20   18   6   5   20   10   18

   16   11   18   17   12   9   20

4. **Draw the beads on the necklaces.**

   a 11 red beads   **b** 15 blue beads   **c** 17 green beads

How did I do?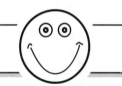

Total

13

More practice? Go to www

Challenge yourself

Put a tick in each necklace with 13 beads.

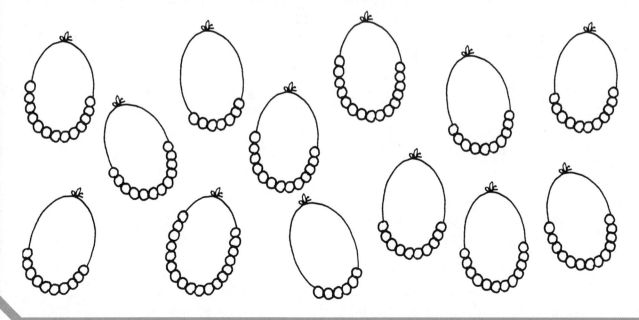

Ordering numbers to 20

Look at the numbers. They go up in **order**.

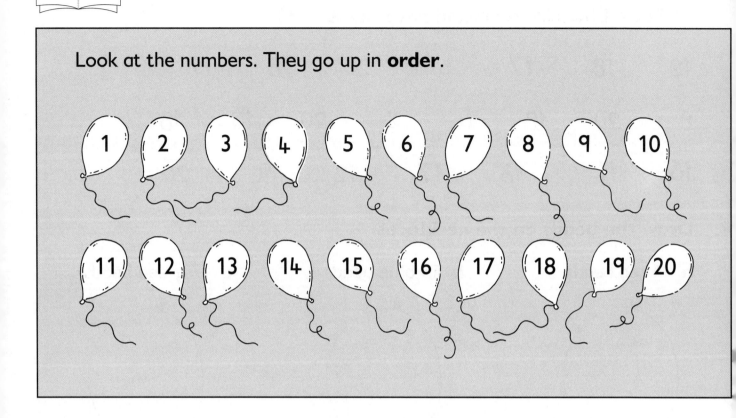

1. **Join the dots to make the shapes. Start at 1. Use a ruler.**

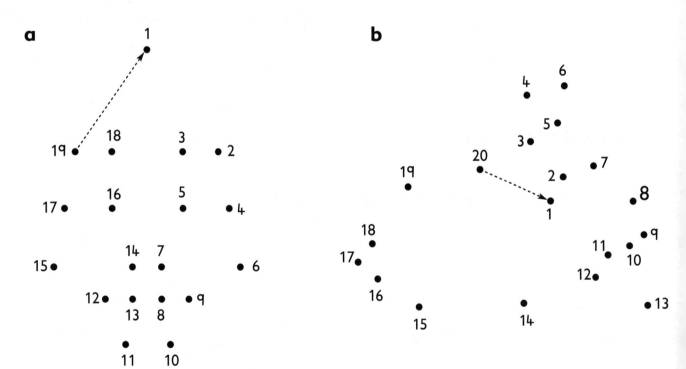

2. **Fill in the missing numbers.**

a

4	5	6	7		9	10	11	12	13	14	15		17	18	19	20

b

6	7	8	9	10	11		13		15	16	17	18		20

c

	6	7	8	9	10	11	12	13	14	15	16	17		19	20

3. **Which number comes first when you count in order?**

a 12 or 6? __6__   **b** 14 or 15? _____

c 20 or 18? _____   **d** 17 or 9? _____

e 13 or 11? _____   **f** 9 or 10? _____

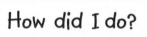 How did I do? _____ _____

Total /10

More practice? Go to www

Challenge yourself

1	2	3	4	5	6	7	8	9	10	11	12	13	14	15	16	17	18	19	20

Look at the number line.

a Which number comes before 17? _____

b Which number comes after 5? _____

c Which number comes after 13? _____

d Which number comes before 20? _____

e Which number comes after 16? _____

f Which number comes before 10? _____

Lesson 21

Tens and units

Look at the number.

14

T   U

14 is **1 ten** and **4 units**

1. **Fill in the gaps.**

a   12 = = _____ ten _____ units

b   18 = = _____ ten _____ units

c   6 = = _____ tens _____ units

d   15 = = _____ ten _____ units

e   11 = = _____ ten _____ unit

2. Draw the tens and units and fill in the gaps.

a 14 = 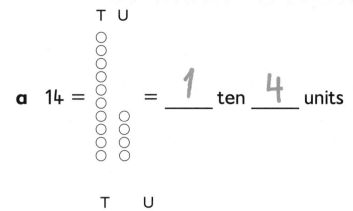 = __1__ ten __4__ units

b 17 = 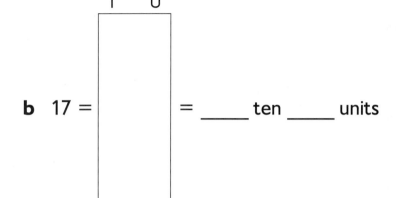 = _____ ten _____ units

c 8 = = _____ tens _____ units

How did I do?			Total

More practice? Go to www

Challenge yourself

Which number is the same as ...

a one ten and seven units? _____   b one ten and one unit? _____

c no tens and three units? _____   d one ten and nine units? _____

Counting in steps of 1 and 10

These numbers **go on 1** at a time.   8 9 10 11 12

These numbers **go back 1** at a time.   12 11 10 9 8

1. **Write the next two numbers.**

a 3 4 5 6 7 | 8 | 9 |

b 8 7 6 5 4 | | |

c 10 11 12 13 14 | | |

d 19 18 17 16 15 | | |

2. **Answer the questions.**

1	2	3	4	5	6	7	8	9	10	11	12	13	14	15	16	17	18	19	20

a If you count from 11 back to 5 how many numbers do you count? _____

b If you count from 9 on to 13 how many numbers do you count? _____

c If you count from 18 back to 12 how many numbers do you count? _____

d If you count from 8 on to 15 how many numbers do you count? _____

e If you count from 12 back to 3 how many numbers do you count? _____

These numbers **go on 10** at a time.   10 20 30 40 50

These numbers **go back 10** at a time.   50 40 30 20 10

Use the 100 square to help you answer the questions on this page.

3. Write the next two numbers.

1	2	3	4	5	6	7	8	9	10
11	12	13	14	15	16	17	18	19	20
21	22	23	24	25	26	27	28	29	30
31	32	33	34	35	36	37	38	39	40
41	42	43	44	45	46	47	48	49	50
51	52	53	54	55	56	57	58	59	60
61	62	63	64	65	66	67	68	69	70
71	72	73	74	75	76	77	78	79	80
81	82	83	84	85	86	87	88	89	90
91	92	93	94	95	96	97	98	99	100

a 40 50 60 70 | 80 | 90 |

b 10 20 30 40 | | |

c 60 50 40 30 | | |

d 90 80 70 60 | | |

How did I do?   ___ ___

Total
/11

More practice? Go to www

Challenge yourself

Write the answer.

a Start with 40. Count on 2 tens.

| |

b Start with 70. Count back 4 tens.

| |

c Start with 20. Count on 3 tens.

| |

d Start with 90. Count back 6 tens.

| |

1 or 10 more or less

As numbers go up, they are **one more** than the number before.

•	••	•••	••••	•••••	•••••	••••••	••••••	•••••	•••••
1	2	3	4	5	6	7	8	9	10
11	12	13	14	15	16	17	18	19	20

1. Answer these questions.

a   Which numbers are less than 3? _____ _____

b   Which numbers are 1 and 2 more than 18? _____ _____

2. Write the number.

a   1 more than 9.   _____   b   1 less than 15.   _____

c   1 more than 17.   _____   d   1 less than 20.   _____

e   1 more than 6.   _____   f   1 less than 2.   _____

3. Fill in the missing numbers.

a

4	5		7	8	9		11		13	14	15

b

15	14	13		11	10		8	7	6		4

c

	18	17	16			13	12	11	10		8

4. **Fill in the gaps.**

1 + 10 = _11_   2 + 10 = _____   3 + 10 = _____

4 + 10 = _____   5 + 10 = _____   6 + 10 = _____

7 + 10 = _____   8 + 10 = _____   9 + 10 = _____

10 + 10 = _____

What happens when we add 10 to each number? _____

_____

5. **Answer the questions.**

a What number is 10 more than 2? _____

b What number is 10 less than 17? _____

c What number is 10 more than 8? _____

d What number is 10 less than 11? _____

How did I do?      Total /25

More practice? Go to **www**

Challenge yourself

a A ruler costs 8p. A toy car costs 10p more.
How much does a car cost? _____

b Dan has 5p. Nina has 10p more.
How much does Nina have? _____

c It is 16th May.
It was Aimee's birthday 10 days ago.
What date is Aimee's birthday on? _____

			May			
S	M	T	W	T	F	S
1	2	3	4	5	6	7
8	9	10	11	12	13	14
15	16	17	18	19	20	21
22	23	24	25	26	27	28
29	30	31				

Counting in steps to 20

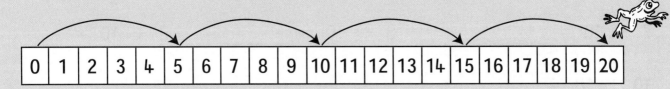

Look at the frog. It is jumping along the number line.

The frog jumps up **5 numbers** each time.

1. **How many numbers does the frog jump up each time?**

a

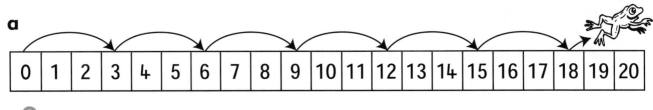

_3_ numbers each time

b

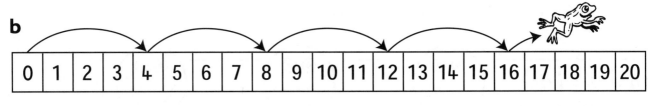

_____ numbers each time

c

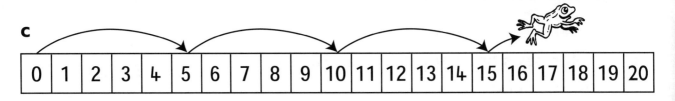

_____ numbers each time

d

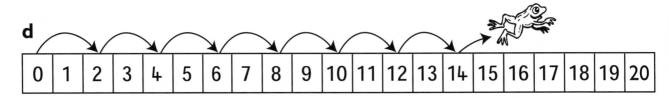

_____ numbers each time

2. **Finish the jumps, keeping them the same.**

Colour the numbers the frog lands on.

a

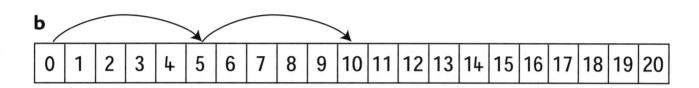

| 0 | 1 | 2 | 3 | 4 | 5 | 6 | 7 | 8 | 9 | 10 | 11 | 12 | 13 | 14 | 15 | 16 | 17 | 18 | 19 | 20 |

b

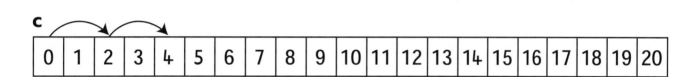

| 0 | 1 | 2 | 3 | 4 | 5 | 6 | 7 | 8 | 9 | 10 | 11 | 12 | 13 | 14 | 15 | 16 | 17 | 18 | 19 | 20 |

c

| 0 | 1 | 2 | 3 | 4 | 5 | 6 | 7 | 8 | 9 | 10 | 11 | 12 | 13 | 14 | 15 | 16 | 17 | 18 | 19 | 20 |

3. **Which numbers come next?**

a 3 6 9 _____ _____   **b** 5 10 _____ _____

c 4 8 _____ _____   **d** 6 8 _____ _____

e 9 12 _____ _____

Total

How did I do?

/11

More practice? Go to www

Challenge yourself

a Colour red the numbers that go up by 3 each time. Start at 3.

1	2	3	4	5
6	7	8	9	10
11	12	13	14	15
16	17	18	19	20

b Colour green the numbers that go up by 5 each time. Start at 5.

Look at the patterns you have made.

Odd and even numbers to 20

Look at these numbers.

1   3   5   7   9

The first number is 1. The numbers go up two at a time.
These are **odd numbers**.

Look at these numbers.

2   4   6   8   10

The first number is 2. The numbers go up two at a time.
These are **even numbers**.

1. **Here is a number line to 10.**

1	2	3	4	5	6	7	8	9	10

   a Colour the even numbers red.

   b Colour the odd numbers green.

2. **Cirle the even numbers.**

2   7   1   4   8

5   9   6   10   3

3. **a** What is the first odd number? _____

b What is the second even number? _____

c What is the third odd number? _____

d What is the first even number? _____

e What is the fifth odd number? _____

4. **Here is a number line to 20.**

0	1	2	3	4	5	6	7	8	9	10	11	12	13	14	15	16	17	18	19	20

a Colour the odd numbers blue.

b Colour the even numbers yellow.

5. **Which numbers come next?**

a 6 8 10 12 _____ _____   **b** 9 11 13 15 _____ _____

How did I do? _____ _____ _____

Total _____ / 12

More practice? Go to www

Challenge yourself

Are these numbers odd or even?

a 6 _____   **b** 17 _____

c 20 _____   **d** 1 _____

e 13 _____   **f** 18 _____

g 12 _____   **h** 9 _____

Number sequences

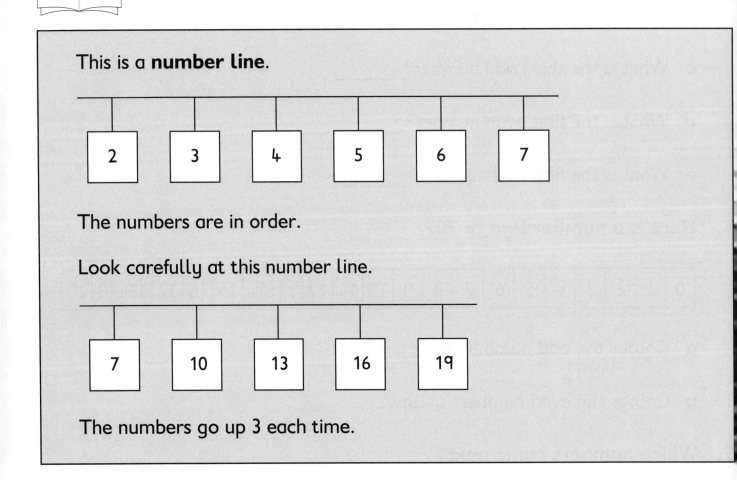

This is a **number line**.

| 2 | 3 | 4 | 5 | 6 | 7 |

The numbers are in order.

Look carefully at this number line.

| 7 | 10 | 13 | 16 | 19 |

The numbers go up 3 each time.

1. **Fill in the missing numbers.**

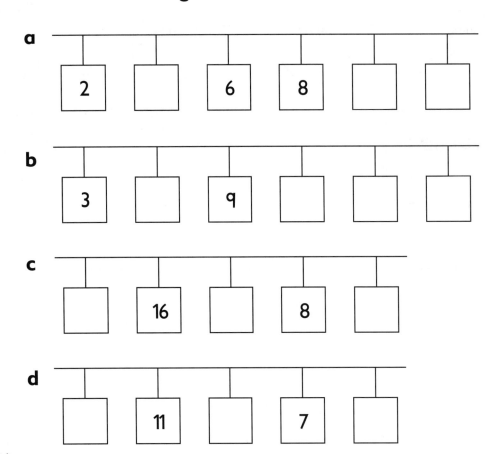

a | 2 | | 6 | 8 | | |

b | 3 | | 9 | | | |

c | | 16 | | 8 | |

d | | 11 | | 7 | |

2. Which numbers have been swapped round?

Put a circle around them.

0	1	2	3	5	4	6	7	8	9	10	11	12	13	14	15	16	18	17	19	20

3. Put these numbers in order, the smallest first.

a 6 2 17 10   _2_ _6_ _10_ _17_

b 5 3 9 6   _3_ ___ ___ ___

c 7 19 12 8   ___ ___ ___ ___

d 20 5 14 9   ___ ___ ___ ___

e 1 13 7 19   ___ ___ ___ ___

f 16 8 3 13   ___ ___ ___ ___

How did I do?

Total
/10

More practice? Go to www

Challenge yourself

Make your own number pattern.

It needs to go up in steps of 4 but also must have the number 6 in it!

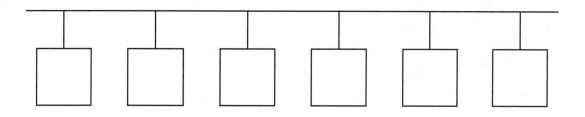

Estimating

1. **a** Don't count, just guess how many dogs there are here. _____

Now count them. _____

b Guess how many birds there are here. _____

Now count them. _____

2. **Make your estimation and count only to check your answers.**

a Estimate how many ducks
are in the pond. _____
Are you right? _____

b Estimate how many chickens
are in the pen. _____
Are you right? _____

c Estimate how many
cows are in the field. _____
Are you right? _____

d Estimate how many
ladybirds are in the jar. _____
Are you right? _____

How did I do?

Total

6

More practice? Go to www

Challenge yourself

Estimate whether there are enough apples for the donkeys to have one each. Put a circle around 'Yes' or 'No'.

Yes   No   **Are you right?**

59

Time – half past

This clock shows half past 4.

The **big hand** is pointing at the 6.

The **small hand** is pointing halfway past the 4.

It tells us we are **halfway** through the hour.

1. **What is the time?**

a   half past _____

b   half past _____

c   half past _____

d   half past _____

e   half past _____

f   half past _____

2. Draw the small hand on the clocks.

a half past 9

b half past 3

c half past 1

d half past 11

e half past 6

f half past 7

How did I do?

Total

12

More practice? Go to **www**

Challenge yourself

It is half past 2.

a What time will it be in half an hour's time? _____

b What time was it 2 hours ago? _____

c In how many hours will it be half past 4? _____

1. **Draw the beads on the necklaces.**

a 12 beads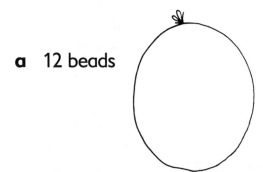

b 18 beads

2. **Which number comes first when you count in order?**

a 19 or 17? _____

b 11 or 13? _____

3. **Draw the tens and units and fill in the gaps.**

a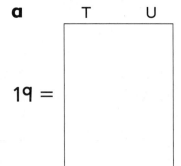

19 = _____ ten _____ units

b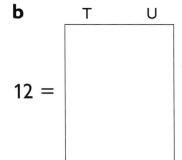

12 = _____ ten _____ units

4. **Write the answer.**

a Start with 5. Count on 6. _____

b Start with 17. Count back 4. _____

5. **a** What number is 10 more than 8? _____

b What number is 10 less than 13? _____

6. **Fill in the missing numbers.**

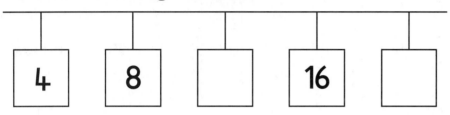

7. **Write 2 odd numbers.**

_____ _____

8. **Put these numbers in order, largest first.**

5 19 2 14   _____ _____ _____ _____

9. **Estimate how many apples there are on the tree.** _____

Now count them. _____

10. **What is the time?**

a

 half past _____

b

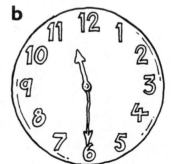 half past _____

Total

/16

More practice? Go to

Try the 6–7 years book

Read and write numbers to 100

100 =

100 = 10 tens

46 =

46 = 4 tens 6 units

1. Colour in the correct number of tens and units.
   The first one has been done for you.

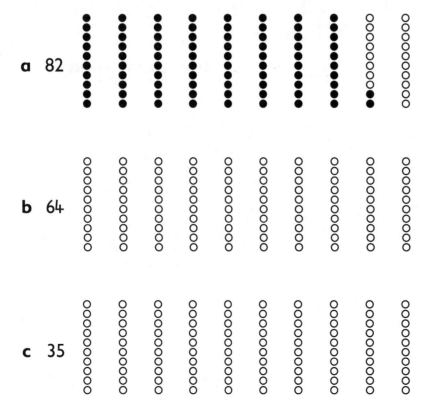

a 82

b 64

c 35